NOAH TAKES TWO

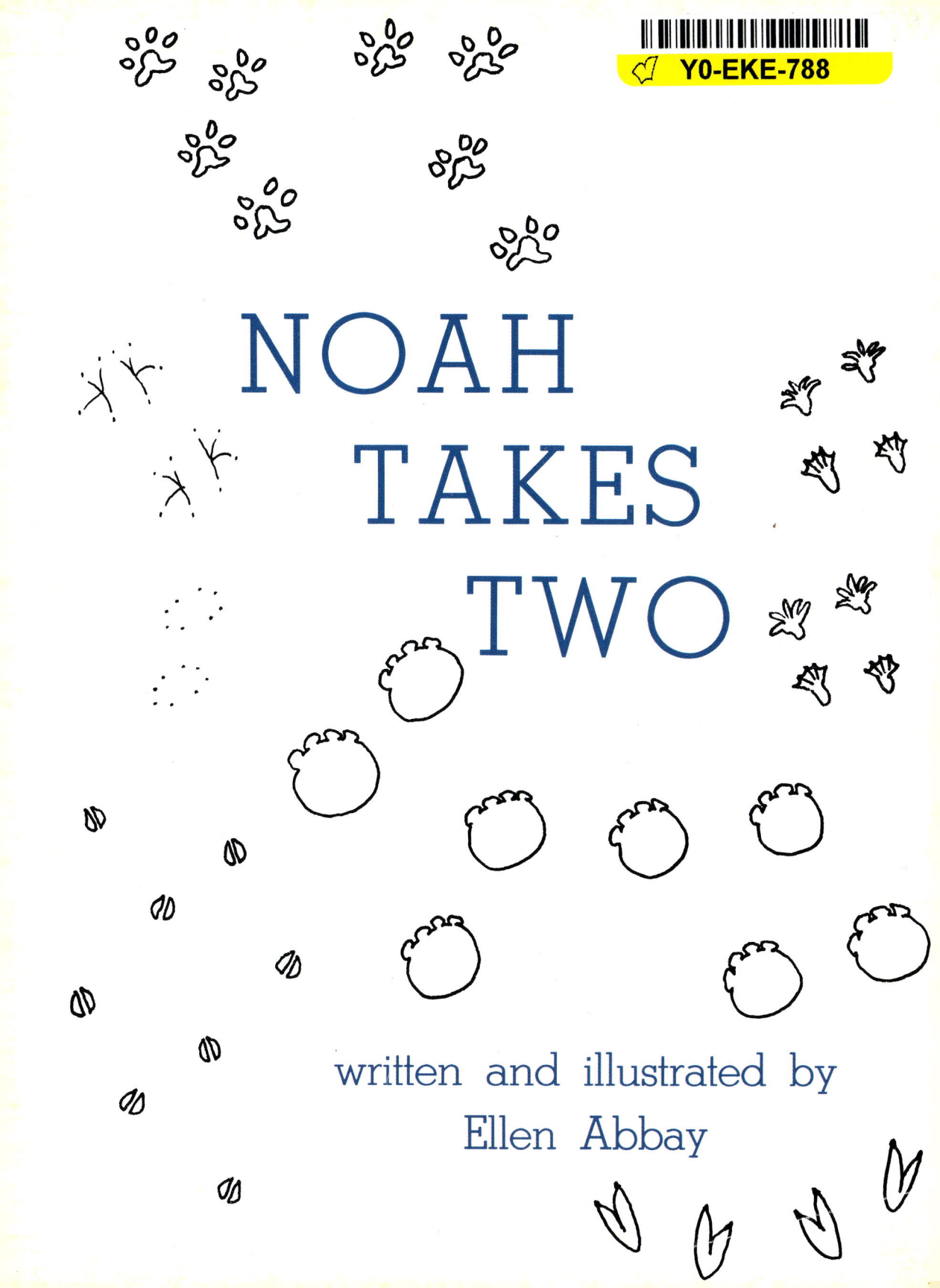

written and illustrated by
Ellen Abbay

Dedicated to my children
Rob, Will, & Mary Ellen

Kudzu & Co.

Publications Nurturing Creative Growth

P.O. BOX 415
WALLS, MISSISSIPPI 38680

© Copyright 1985
ISBN 0-9615015-0-2
Library of Congress Catalog Card Number: 85-80406

Tens and hundreds of years ago
      God promised a mighty rain.
It would flood the earth and wash away
      Every building and tree and lane.

He said it would rain for days and nights,
      For a month and ten days more,
Til water covered the whole wide world
      And the waves could touch no shore.

Men scorned the warnings and didn't listen,
    Only Noah prepared to obey;
So God chose him to survive the flood
    In an ark that would float away.

Noah would build this ship of wood
To be long and very wide,
Big enough to comfortably hold
Hundreds of people inside.

But people were not the passenger list
    On this ark that Noah created.
Two of each animal on the earth
       Would ride, safe til the waters abated.

So Noah sawed and Noah hammered,
    And he chopped and hammered some more;
And he fashioned a ship that was roomy and dry,
    And tall with a double wide door.

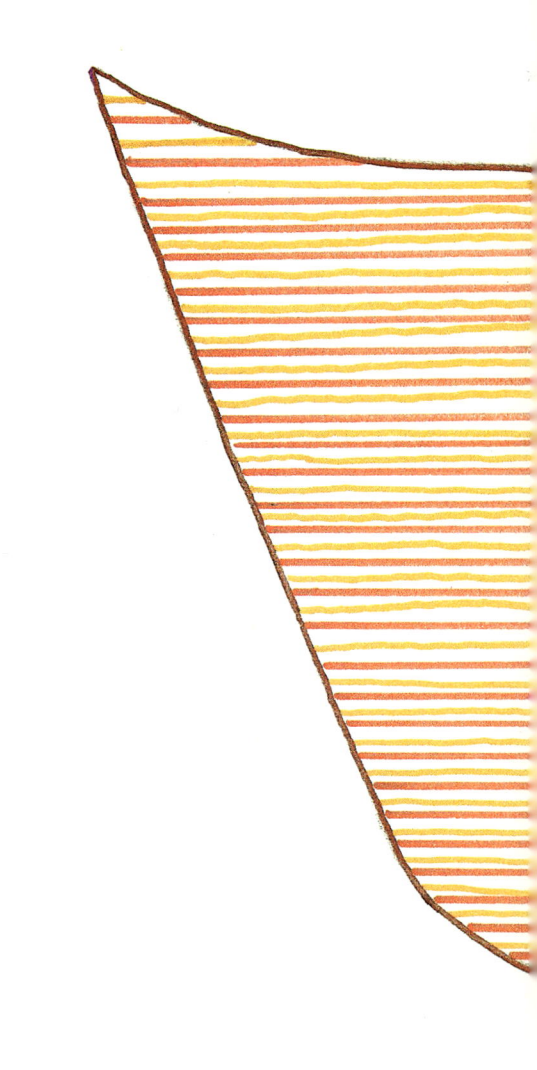

Into this door came his wife and sons
    And they watched with fascination,
As pairs of animals came marching in . . .
    The longest parade in creation.

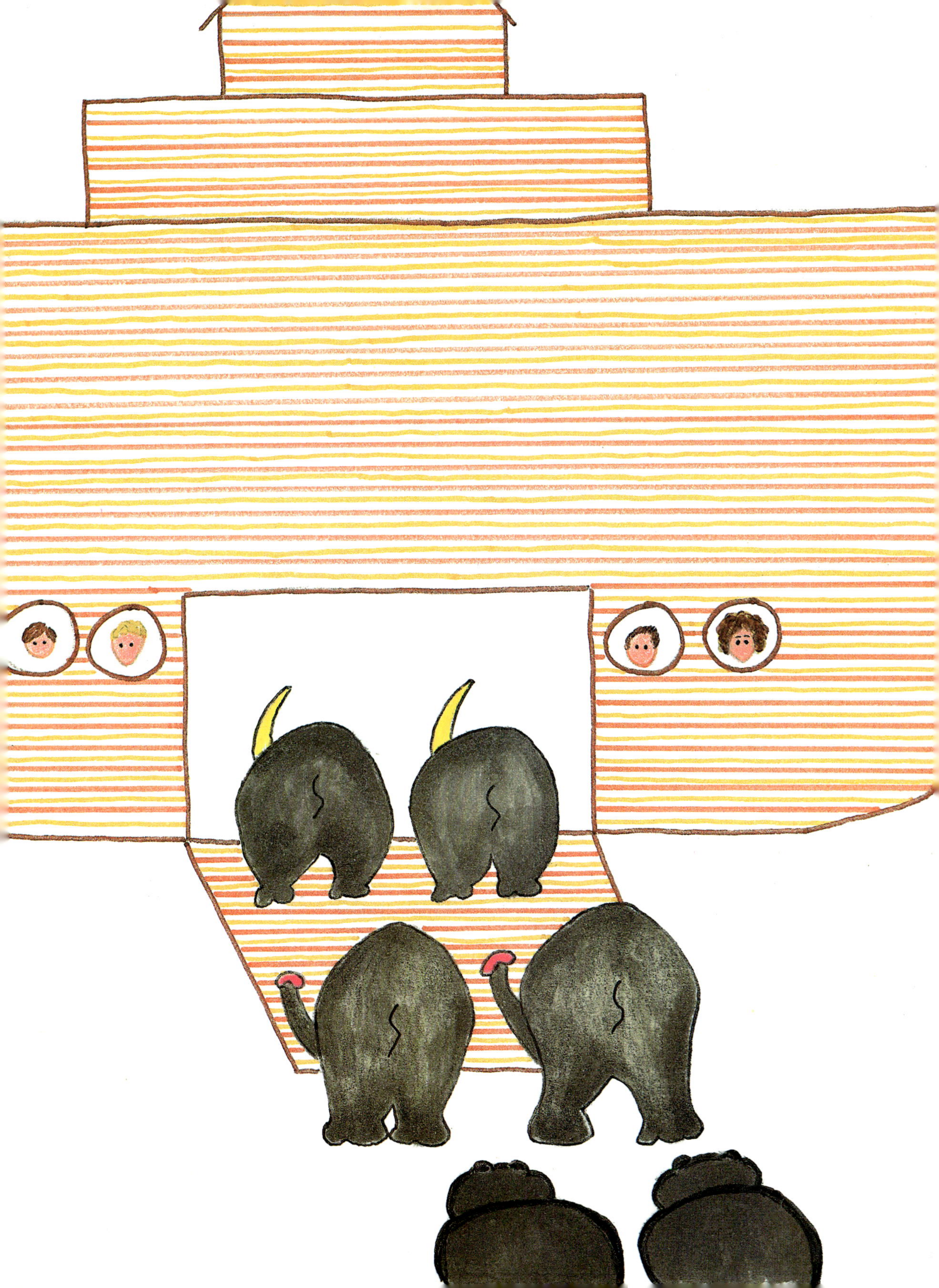

The heaviest animals came on first
    So their weight would balance the ride.
Two leathery rhinos pointed the way,
    Their horns uplifted to guide.

The hippos opened big wide mouths
    For a toothy yawn and "hello",
Then waddled on a lazy pace,
    So they could lie down below.

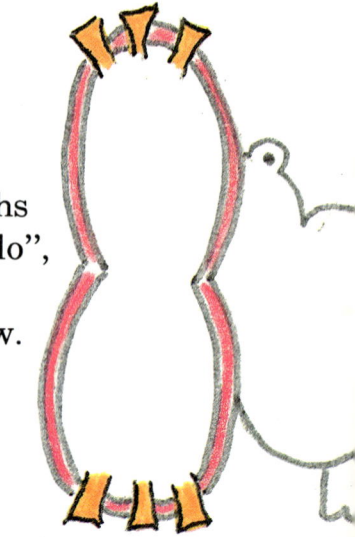

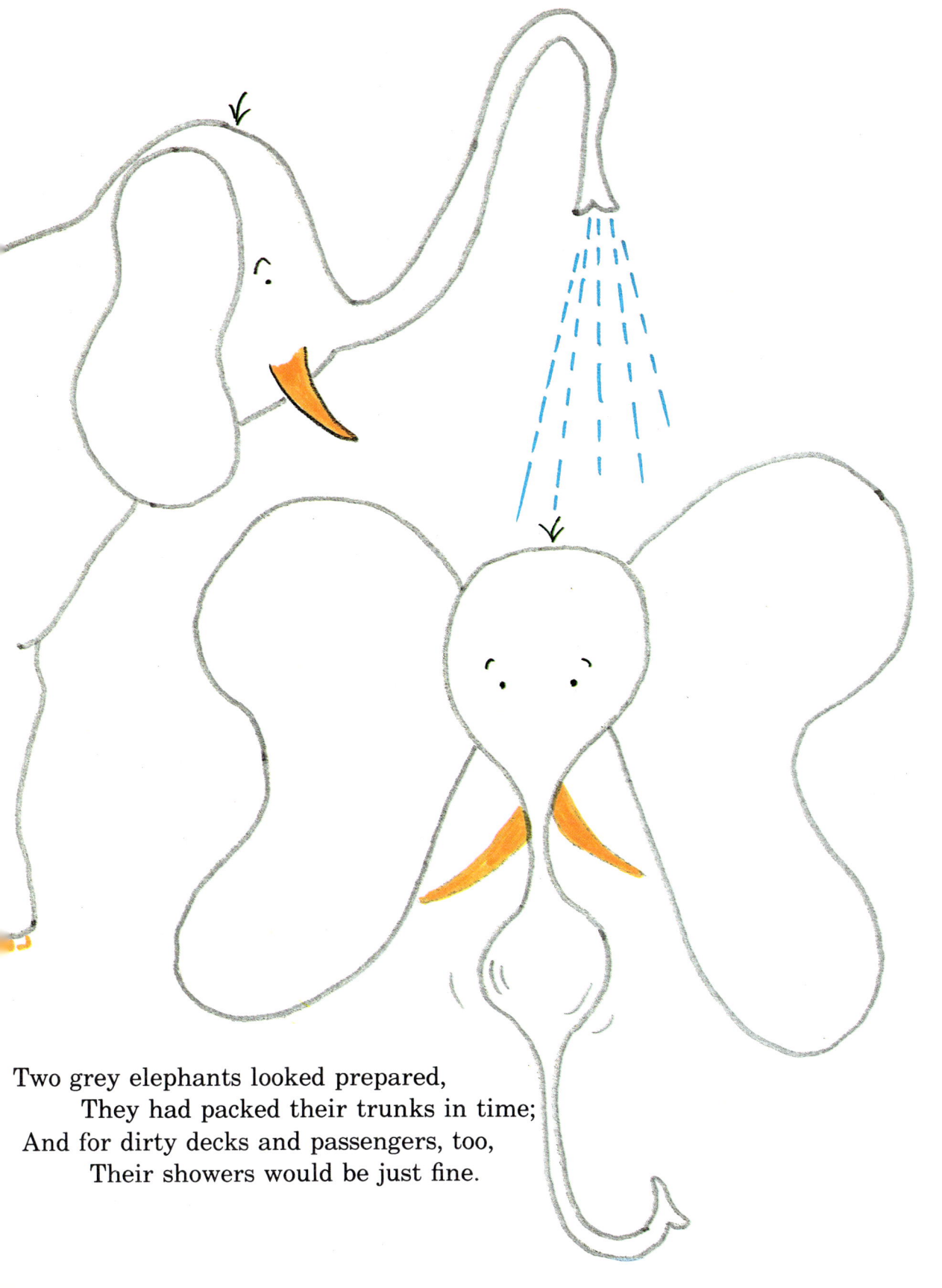

Two grey elephants looked prepared,
　　They had packed their trunks in time;
And for dirty decks and passengers, too,
　　Their showers would be just fine.

And other animals brought supplies,
   That could help during weeks at sea;
The beaver's sharp teeth could cut wood or a rope,
   As easy as easy could be.

The broad beaver tail could be used as a hammer,
The woodpecker brought his drill;
The goat's appetite was the garbage disposal,
And the moose had coat racks to fill.

The shaggy sheep could give wool for warmth,
And the cows carried gallons of cream;
The porcupines brought plenty of needles
So someone could sew a seam.

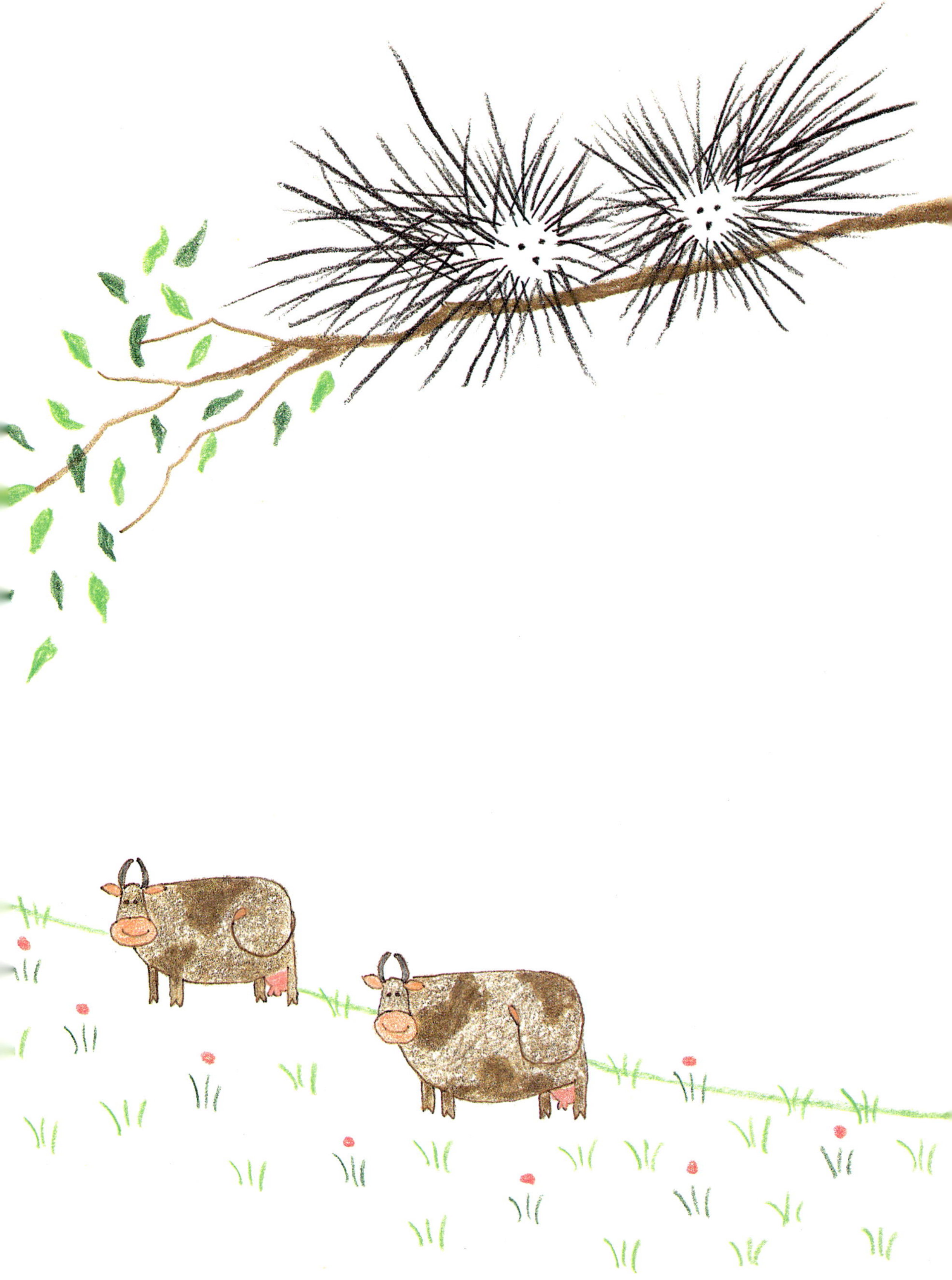

The turkey feathers made lovely quill pens,
    The squids would provide the ink:
The anteaters came prepared to vacuum,
    The camels stored water to drink.

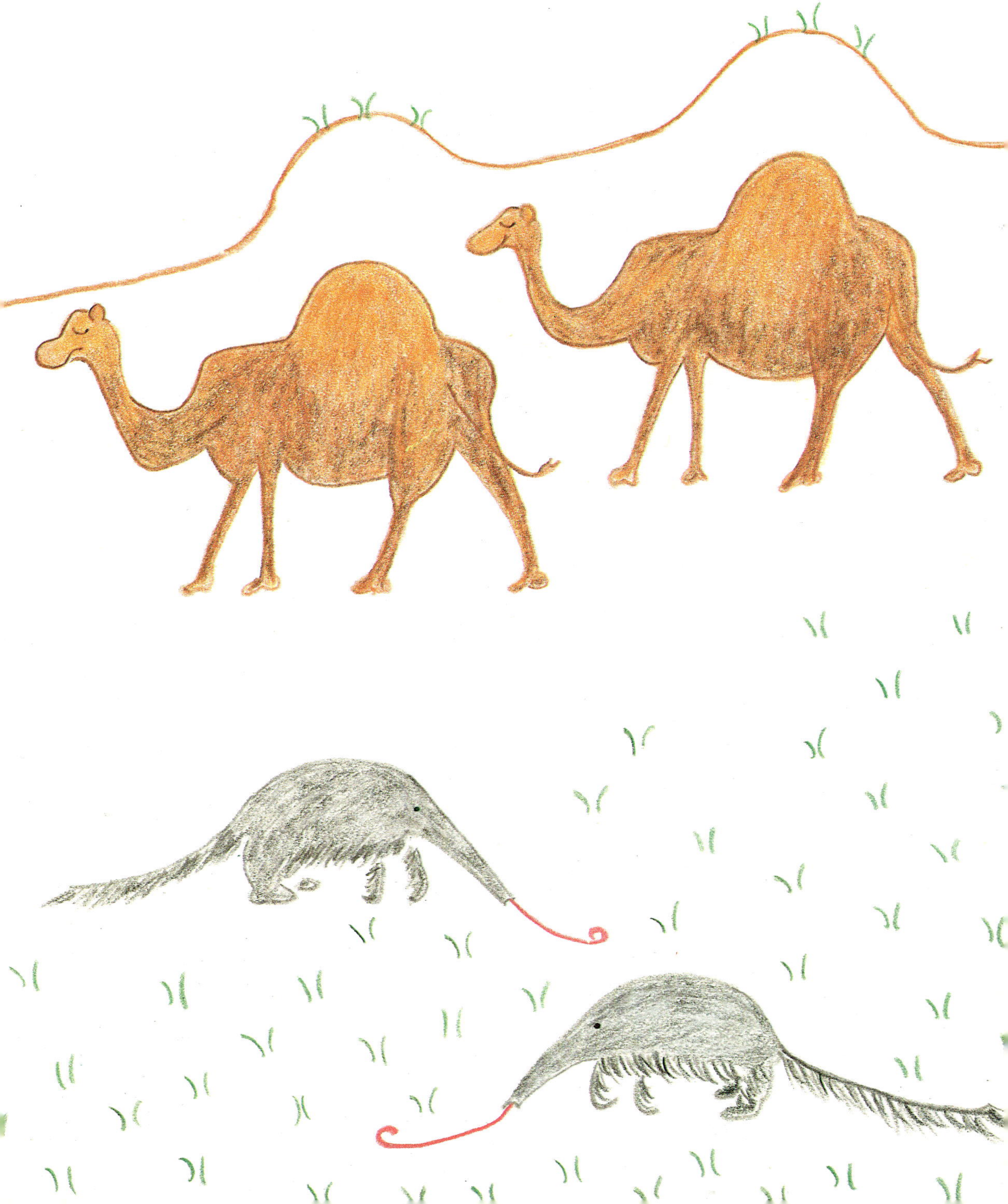

The squirrel's fluffy tail made a flexible duster,
    And snake bellies polished the floors;
Barn swallows mudded up any cracks,
    In the sides or over the doors.

The fireflies together could light up the night,
Black spiders could weave a curtain;
Bunnies' cotton-tail puffs could apply First Aid,
To scrapes or wounds that were hurtin'.

Giraffe's long neck could reach up through the roof,
    A periscope elevation.
He'd look forward & backward & side to side,
    So nifty for navigation.

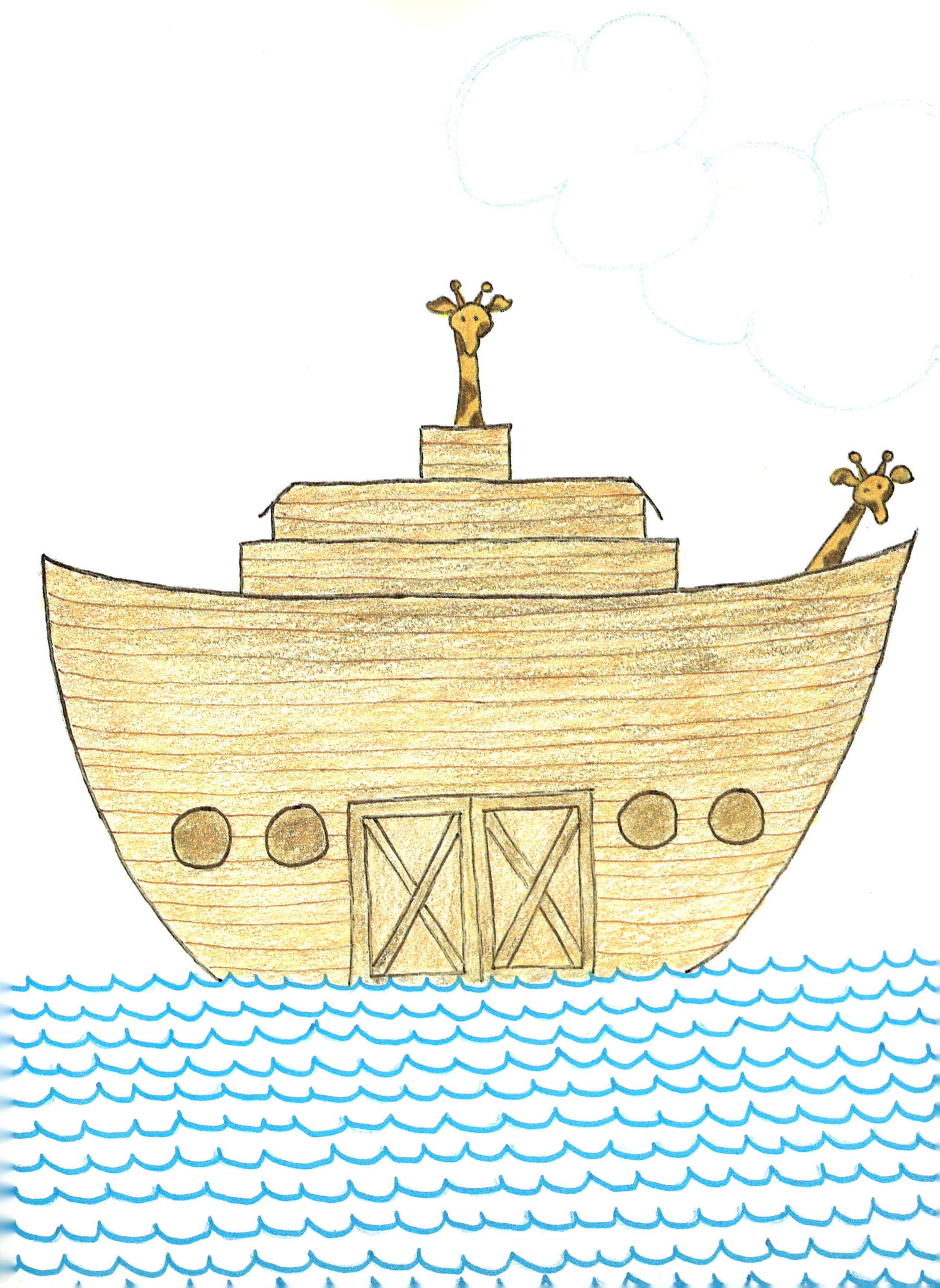

As animals marched in two by two,
    (The original fashion parade),
So many outfits and styles appeared,
    All natural and custom-made.

The zebras and tigers wore stripes up and down,
    (To show which way they were goin').
The leopards wore spots they could never change,
    And the peacocks had all colors showin'.

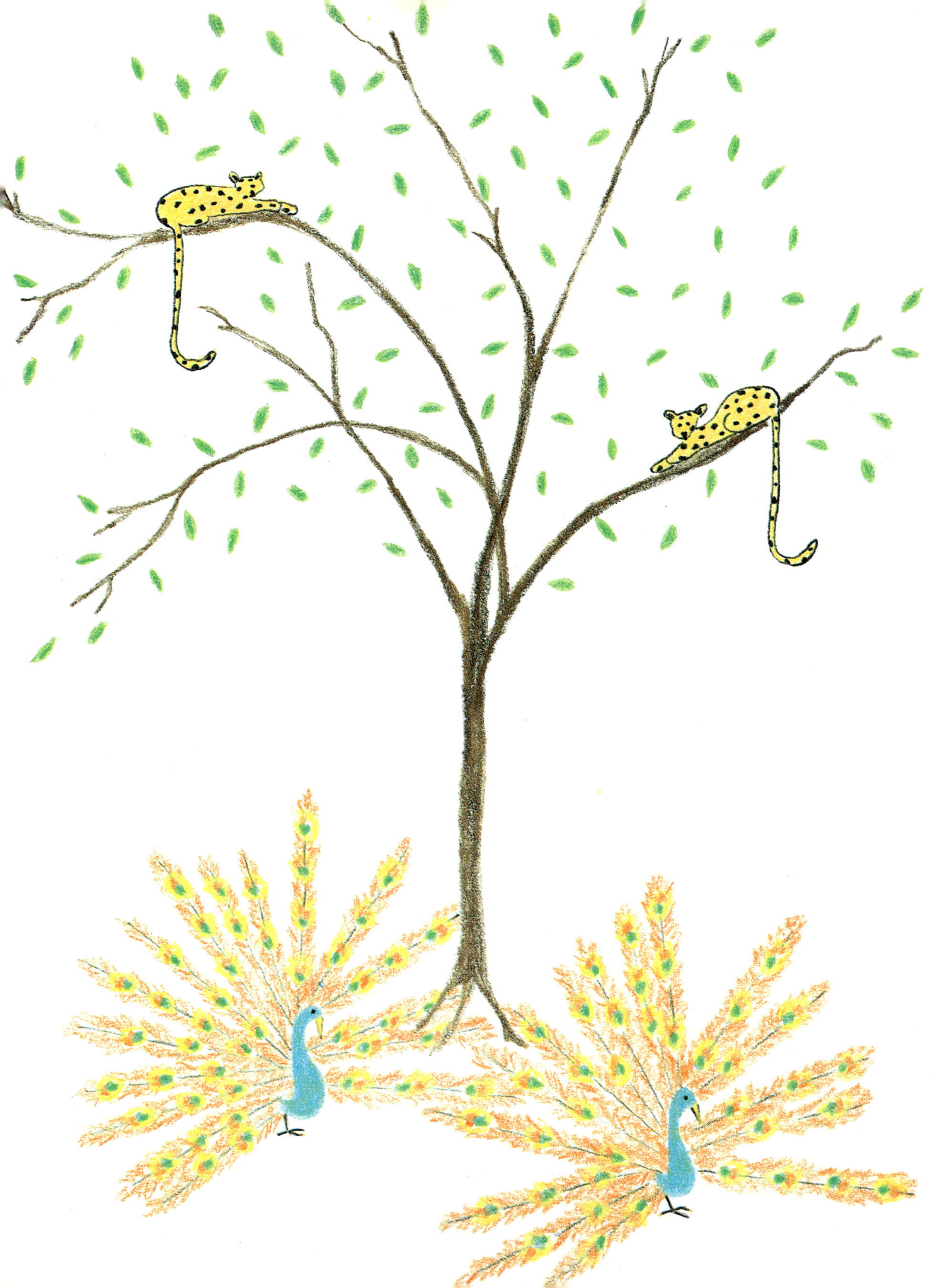

The kangaroos showed pockets in front,
    The roosters wore floppy hats;
The bears were wrapped in long fur coats,
    Masks hid coons and Siamese cats.

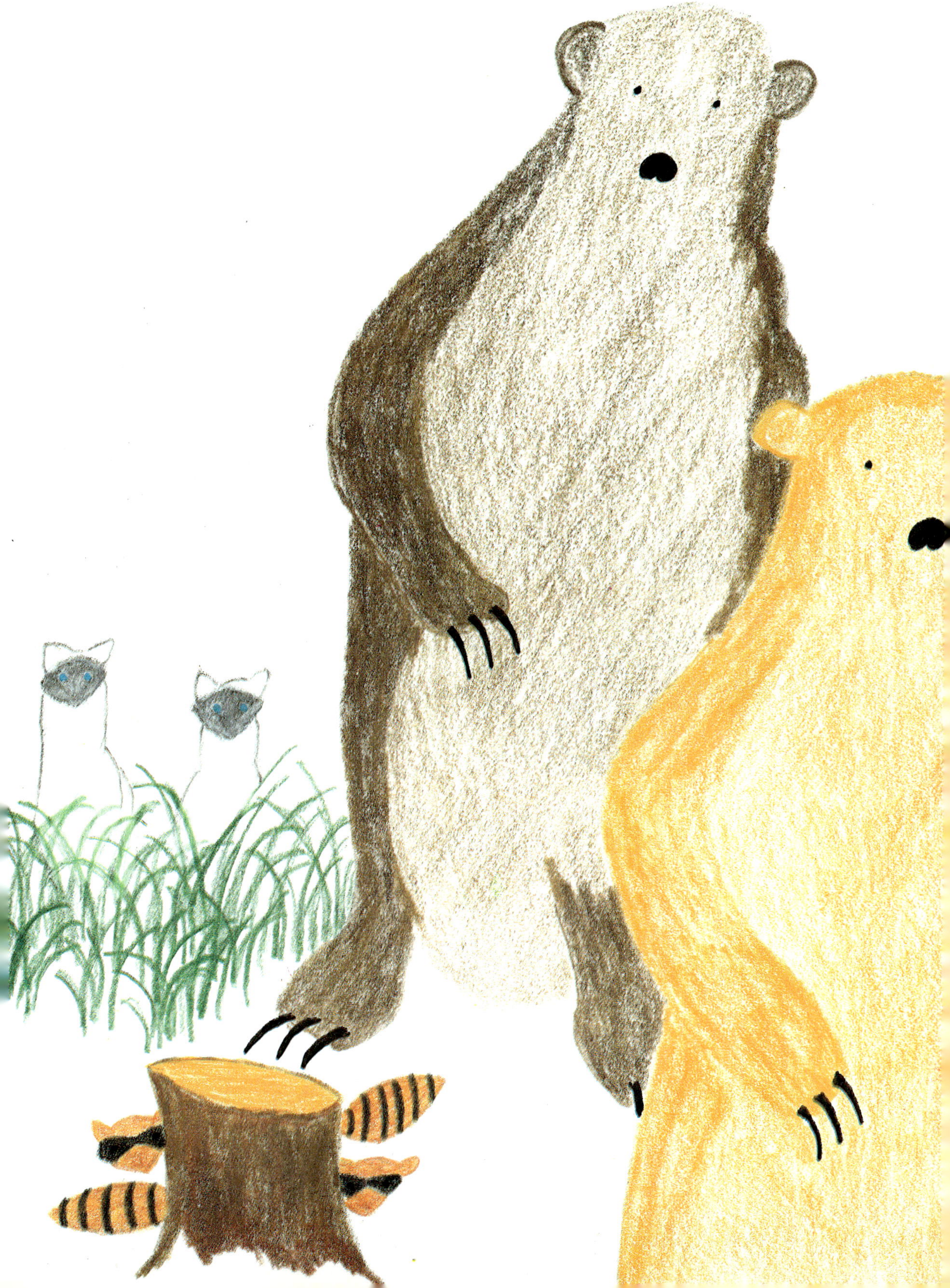

The penguins looked sharp in black & white tux;
    More casual the ostrich must be —
The short, fluffy dress this 'big bird' wore,
    Did not even reach to her knee.

The dogs were perfect, as 'Man's Best Friend',
    To make each feel at home on this ride;
No one could be lonely or scared or upset,
    With a dog wagging close at his side.

And for entertainment on this long trip,
    Armadillos would roll into balls;
Alligator teeth made a grand piano,
    So music could fill the halls.

The yellow canaries could sing any song,
    The pig's curly tail made a slinky;
Jellyfish became silly-putty for fun,
    But the skunks played a game that was stinky ! !

They could watch chameleons change colors again,
From green into yellow then brown;
Or play possum, a game the possum invented,
To fake sleeping while lying down.

Both the monkeys were really swingin',
    As they flipped through the rafters new;
They copied each other in every scratch —
    The first "Monkey see, Monkey do."

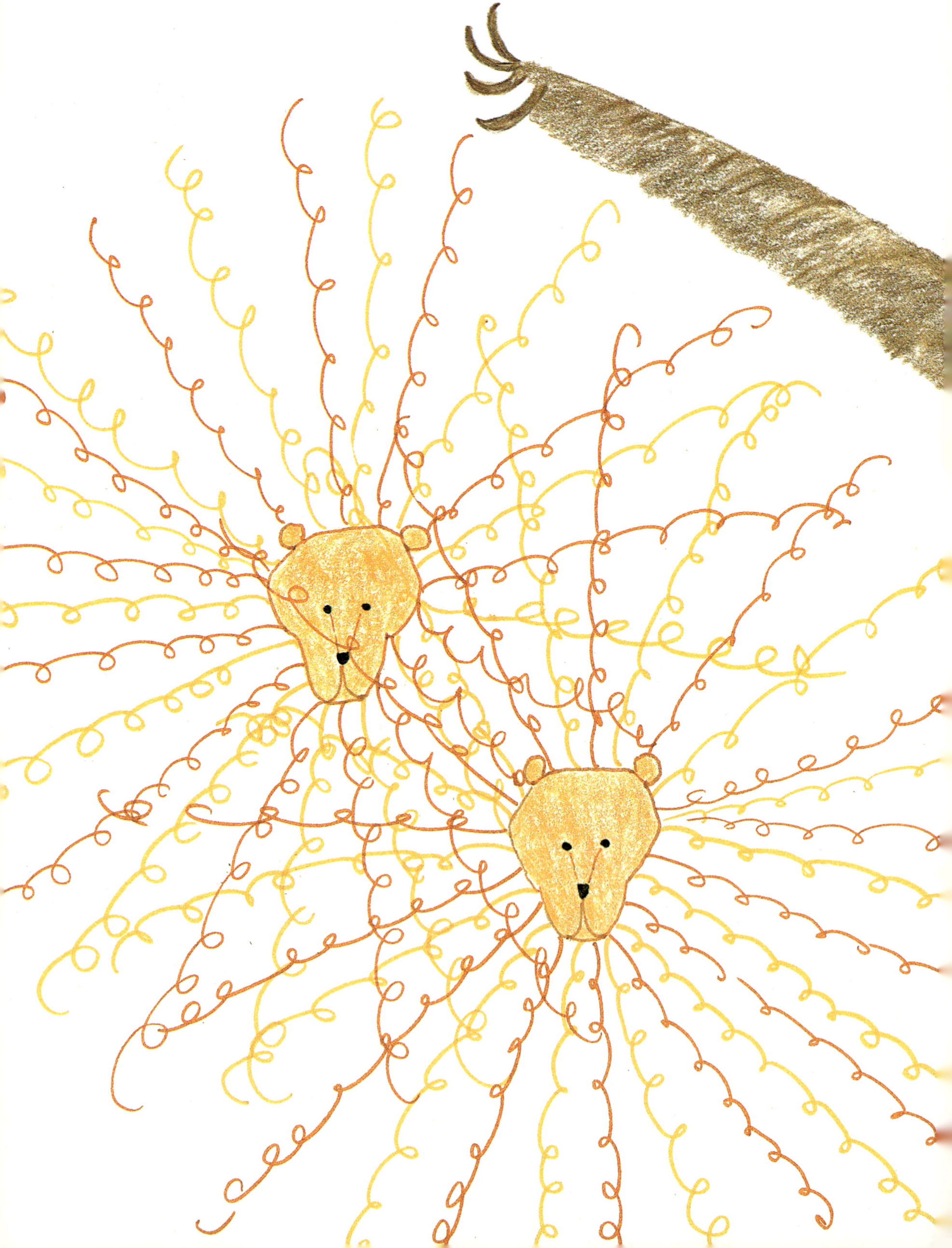

The lions, of course, were the "mane" event,
      With their kingly crowns of hair;
The very bald eagle was jealous for sure,
      But his wings made him king of the air.

"Maybe you can roar, but I can soar,"
      He said to the king of beasts;
"You can protect, and I can inspect . . .
      We can work together, at least."

During weeks of rains and weeks afloat,
    All these animals worked together.
They shared their talents and shared the fun,
    As they waited for sunny weather.

And finally the waters did go down
    And the ark sat upon dry land.
A glorious rainbow showed "never again",
    For this was God's promise to man.

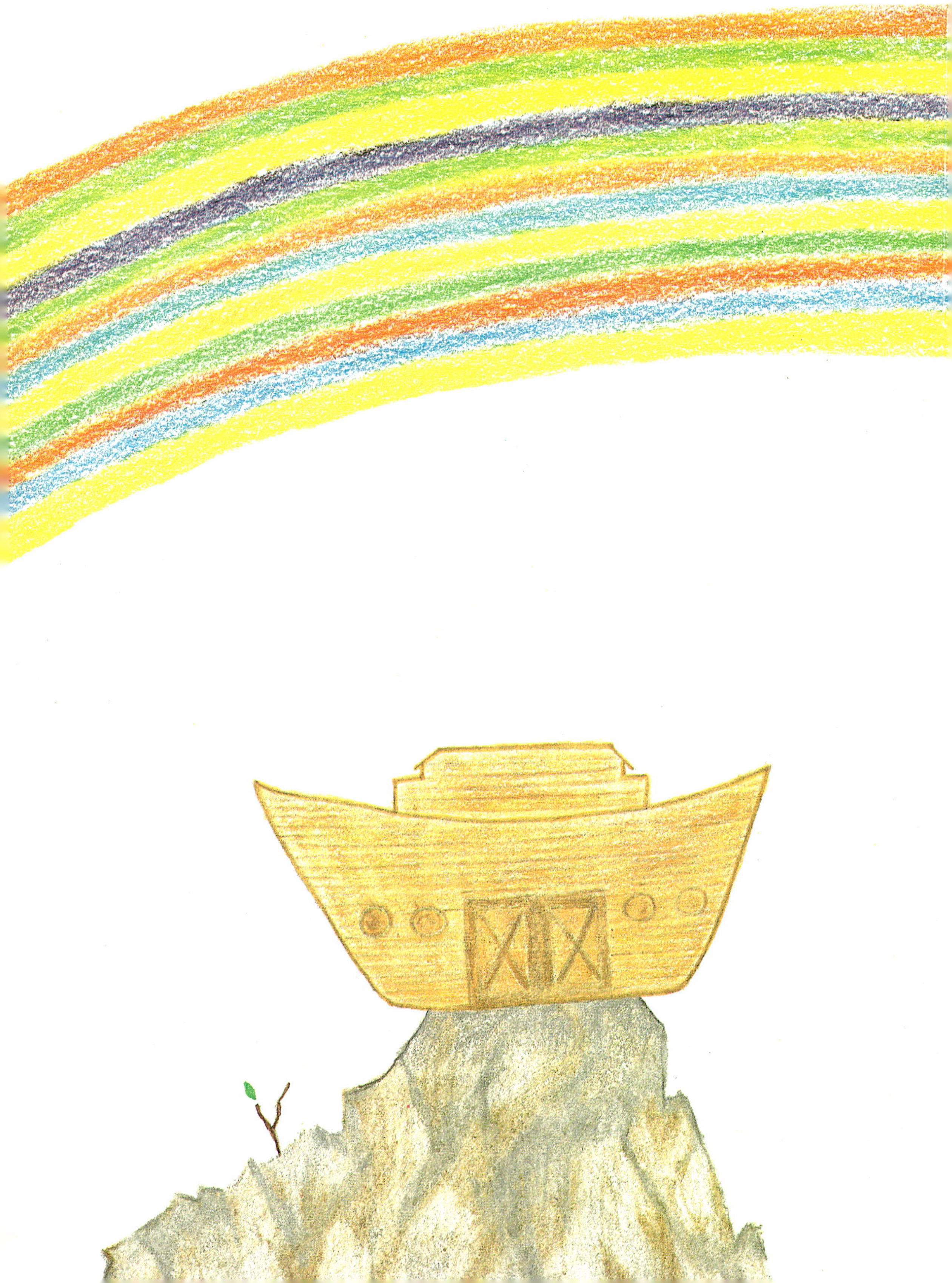

The End . . .

. . . . and a new beginning . . . .